SPARTACUS AND THE SLAVE REVOLT THAT SHOOK THE ROMAN EMPIRE

Edited & Introduced by Christian Høgsbjerg

a Redwords pamphlet

Spartacus and the slave revolt that shook the Roman Empire
A speech by Chris Harman
Introduction by Christion Høgsbjerg
A Redwords pamphlet published September 2024.

Reprinted 2025

ISBN: 978 1 917020 10 7

Redwords is connected to
Bookmarks: The Socialist Bookshop,
1 Bloomsbury Street, London WC1B 3QE
https://bookmarksbookshop.co.uk

Design and production: Roger Huddle
Printed by Halstan & Co. Ltd.

Thanks to David Gilcrist for transferring audio speech to text, and Carol Williams for sub-editing and proofreading.

Chris Harman, was a revolutionary Marxist, a leading member of the Socialist Workers Party, writer, editor, speaker and teacher; born 8 November 1942; died 7 November 2009.

CHRIS HARMAN

CONTENTS

Acknowledgements 7 | Introduction 9

SPARTACUS | 25

ACKNOWLEDGEMENTS AND A NOTE ON THE TRANSCRIPTION

THE SPEECH REPRODUCED in this volume was delivered on 5 July 1998 by Chris Harman for a meeting at 'Marxism 1998' in London. Originally titled 'Spartacus and the Battle of Petelia', it reflects the last battle in 71 BCE in which Spartacus was finally defeated and killed as he tried to cut his way through to the Roman general Crassus. The meeting was the first in a course of meetings at Marxism festival that year asking 'Did these battles change history?', and was followed by talks by others on 'Naseby and the English Revolution', 'Culloden and the Jacobite cause', 'Valmy and the French Revolution', 'Gettysburg and the fate of the Confederacy', 'The Russian army and the Russian Revolution' and 'The Tet Offensive'. The transcription is taken from the Bookmarks SoundCloud series, and I am indebted to the Bookmarks team and in particular to Dave Gilchrist for his help in making this and a basic transcript of Chris's speech available to me. With respect to my transcription, it should be noted that there are minor changes to style, one or two corrections to dates (for example where Chris had mixed up BC and AD, which I have at the same time updated to BCE and CE), and I have added subheadings to help break up the text where appropriate. There is a section midway in the recording where Chris realises he is pushed for time and states that he will have to very briefly paraphrase three pages of text. It has, however, been possible to bring out some of the additional rich detail Chris had perhaps planned to include when he delivered it by using his original notes. Simply titled 'Spartacus', his notes are replete with references to the research he had undertaken, and these have been added, where appropriate, as footnotes to the main text. I am also indebted to Talat Ahmed, Ursla Hawthorne, Roger Huddle, Steve Roskams and Nic Watts.

Christian Høgsbjerg, April 2024

INTRODUCTION / CHRISTIAN HØGSBJERG

'THE WAR OF SPARTACUS AND THE SLAVES was the most just war in History; perhaps the only just war in History.'[1] So declared Voltaire in 1770 in his entry on 'Slavery' in the *Encyclopédie*, indicative of the new-found interest in Spartacus in Europe during the mid-eighteenth century, amid the rise of the Enlightenment. The War was actually a rebellion, a heroic rebellion, led by Spartacus, a gladiator from Thrace (Bulgaria), against the Roman Empire which incredibly, lasted for almost two years, from 73 to 71 BCE.

Yet few of Voltaire's readers among the European philosophical establishment would have made any direct link between this new-found republican admiration for a slave revolt in the ancient world – at a time of aristocratic despotism and monarchical dictatorship across Europe itself – and the need for new 'just wars' waged against the highly profitable colonial slavery of the eighteenth-century Atlantic world system. The *Histoire philosophique des Deux Indes* (1770), by the Abbé Raynal and Diderot, denounced the barbarity of contemporary Atlantic slavery and predicted that an 'avenger', a 'new Spartacus', could one day arise, but this was written primarily as a warning to colonial slave-holding elites – not a call to arms. Yet

---

[1] F A Ridley, Spartacus: *The Leader of the Roman Slaves* (Ashford: Frank Maitland, 1962), 1. This booklet was originally written in 1944 by Ridley and published as a pamphlet of the Independent Labour Party in Britain. Ridley's work is online: https://www.marxists.org/history/etol/writers/ridley/1944/spartacus/index.htm

slave revolts were already underway across the Atlantic world, and, indeed, just a few months after Bernard-Joseph Saurin's popular play *Spartacus* was staged to acclaim in Paris in February 1760, 'Tacky's Revolt' rocked the British Empire in colonial Jamaica.[2]

When the French Revolution erupted in 1789, the class struggles in ancient Rome took on new resonance, and not only was Saurin's play *Spartacus* re-staged but in 1794 one important French revolutionary, the first modern socialist, Babeuf, took on the name 'Gracchus' after the Gracchus brothers, 'tribunes of the people' in these struggles.[3] Across the French Empire, the enslaved now took the opportunity presented by the French Revolution to make their own bid for 'Liberty, Equality and Fraternity', most notably in the Haitian Revolution of 1791-1804. Many French revolutionaries like Gracchus Babeuf stood in solidarity with the Haitian Revolution, and, under the pressure of that revolution, the Jacobins formally abolished slavery across the French Empire in 1794. In 1796, the new republican governor of French colonial Saint-Domingue, Étienne Laveaux, honoured Toussaint Louverture, his black deputy and a military genius who led an army of former enslaved now fighting the British and Spanish empires, as not just 'the saviour of legitimate authority' in the colony but 'the black Spartacus, the leader announced by the philosopher Raynal to avenge the crimes perpetuated against his race'.

---

2 Sudhir Hazareesingh, Black Spartacus: *The Epic Life of Toussaint Louverture* (London: Allan Lane, 2020), 33. For a fascinating discussion of representations of Spartacus in the West in the early modern period, see Brent D. Shaw, 'Spartacus before Marx,' Princeton, Stanford Working Papers in *Classics* (2005), https://www.princeton.edu/~pswpc/pdfs/shaw/110516.pdf. See also Brent D. Shaw, *Spartacus and the Slave Wars: A Brief History with Documents* (Boston: Bedford, 2001). On Tacky's Revolt in Jamaica, see Vincent Brown, *Tacky's Revolt: The Story of an Atlantic Slave War* (Cambridge, Massachusetts: Harvard University Press, 2020).

3 Ian Birchall, *The Spectre of Babeuf* (Basingstoke: Macmillan, 1997), 47. As well as this, as Ridley notes, 'one of the most formidable and internationally known revolutionaries of the stormy era of the French Revolution, the German ex-Jesuit, Adam Weishaupt, wrote under the nom-de-plume of "Spartacus"'. Ridley, *Spartacus, 86.*

As Sudhir Hazareesingh notes of Laveaux's accolade, 'this was the first time Toussaint was publicly likened to Spartacus. Nothing moves as swiftly as revolutionary time, but even he, Louverture probably could not have imagined, when he embraced the slave revolt in 1791, that five years later the governor of Saint-Domingue would be comparing him to such an illustrious Thracian predecessor'. Toussaint Louverture himself, who had apparently read Julius Caesar's *Commentaries on the Gallic War*, seems to have appreciated the comparison to Spartacus, having a bust of Raynal in his offices.[4]

As a mass abolitionist movement took off in early nineteenth century Britain, one young woman, Susanna Strickland, published a short novel, *Spartacus: A Roman Story* in 1822. As Edith Hall and Henry Stead note, Strickland's Spartacus 'is a Christlike Thracian shepherd, whose every thought was "turned on forming some plan for the emancipation of himself and his comrades"'.[5] Strickland would go on to become a leading abolitionist in Britain and, as a member of the Anti-Slavery Society, would work with Mary Prince on her slave narrative, *The History of Mary Prince* (1831). This was the first autobiographical account of a black woman to be published in Britain and the only such account we have of a woman about her horrific experiences under British colonial slavery.[6] Once slavery was abolished across the British Empire, and after the Chartist movement – the first national working class movement fighting for universal suffrage – took

---

[4] Hazareesingh, *Black Spartacus*, 99-100, 327. Fidel Castro, while in prison in 1954, declared how 'the insurrection of black slaves in Haiti' inspired him, and that 'at a time when Napoleon was imitating Caesar, and France resembled Rome, the soul of Spartacus was born in Toussaint Louverture'. For an introduction to the Haitian Revolution, see Paul Foot, *Toussaint Louverture and the Haitian Revolution* (London: Redwords, 2021).

[5] Edith Hall and Henry Stead, *A People's History of the Classics: Class and Greco-Roman Antiquity in Britain and Ireland 1689 to 1939* (London: Routledge, 2020), 395.

[6] Mary Prince, *The History of Mary Prince: A West Indian Slave* (London: Penguin, 2000).

off in Britain from the late 1830s, Spartacus was now hailed for the first time as a 'proletarian' leader, *proletarii* being those without property. For example, the Chartist leader Ernest Jones championed Spartacus in his poem criticizing slavery in America, *The New World* (1848-1850), which Jones republished under a new title, *The Revolt of Hindostan*, in 1857 in solidarity with the Indian uprising against imperialist domination that year.[7]

Amid the violent upheavals involved in nation building during the Italian Risorgimento (1848-1861), the bourgeois revolutionary Giuseppe Garibaldi was compared to Spartacus, including by Raffaello Giovagnoli in a 1874 historical novel *Spartaco* (later made into a silent film). One person who was less impressed by the Garibaldi comparison was Ernest Jones's friend Karl Marx, who in a letter to Engels in 1861 revealed that 'I now read, for recreation in the evenings, Appian's account of the Roman civil wars in the original Greek. A very valuable book ... Spartacus appears as the most capital fellow in the whole of ancient history. Great general (*not* a Garibaldi!), a noble character, a true representative of the ancient proletariat.' Marx had little respect for Pompey, one of the famous Roman generals and later rulers of Rome, who alongside Crassus had brutally put down the Spartacus revolt: 'Pompey is nothing but a turd'.[8] In 1865, in response to a questionnaire, Marx named Spartacus his 'favourite hero'.[9]

As reformist currents grew in the European labour movement in the late nineteenth century, those who believed in 'socialism from above' found Spartacus an awkward figure to admire. The Fabian Society, formed in

---

7 Hall and Stead, *A People's History of the Classics*, 396-97.

8 'Letter from Marx to Engels in Manchester', 27 February 1861, quoted in S.S. Prawer, *Karl Marx and World Literature* (Oxford: Oxford University Press, 1978), 209. See also https://www.marxists.org/archive/marx/works/1861/letters/61_02_27-abs.htm

9 'Karl Marx's "Confession"', 1865, quoted in Prawer, *Karl Marx and World Literature*, 390, see also https://www.marxists.org/archive/marx/works/1865/04/01.htm

Britain in 1884, for example, preferred to draw inspiration from the Roman general Quintus Fabius Maximus Verrucosus Cunctator – 'the delayer' – who avoided a head-on confrontation with Hannibal's powerful armies of Carthage at the time of the Second Punic War in 216 BCE. Yet minority currents of revolutionary socialists, such as William Morris, co-author of *Socialism from the Root Up*, kept alive the memory of Spartacus, for example in a 1890 lecture on ancient Rome:

> Roman civilized society had come to be composed in the main of a privileged class of very rich men, whose business was war, politics and pleasure; and money-making as an instrument of these enjoyments; of their hangers-on forming a vast parasitical army; of a huge population of miserable slaves; and of another population of free men (so-called) kept alive by doles of food, and contented with peoples' palaces in the form of theatrical and gladiatorial shows.

Morris noted that 'the energetic public-spirited Roman' was in reality 'mainly a jailer', and 'the despair of men so treated shook the Roman State in one tremendous slave-mutiny, that of Spartacus, and tormented society for centuries in countless minor mutinies by sea and land...'[10]

A year after the Russian Revolution of 1917, Lenin – who thought the revolutionary socialist should aspire to is to be a 'tribune of the oppressed' – wrote and signed a decree on the list of revolutionaries and public figures who deserved monuments, with Spartacus listed as number one.[11] In the Soviet Union, many sports societies were named after Spartacus, the most famous being Spartak Moscow, which adopted the name in 1935, while in 1954

---

10 William Morris, 'The Development of Modern Society' in Nicholas Salmon (ed.) *William Morris on History* (Sheffield: Sheffield Academic Press, 1996), 113-114.

11 Tariq Ali, *The Dilemmas of Lenin: Terrorism, War, Empire, Love, Revolution* (London: Verso, 2017), 253. Tiberius Gracchus and Brutus were also listed.

the Soviet Armenian composer Aram Khachaturian wrote a famous ballet, *Spartacus*, for which he was awarded a Lenin Prize, and which is still regularly performed by the Bolshoi Ballet.

Most notably, during the horrors of the First World War, in Germany, the Spartakusbund or Spartacus League had been formed and officially appeared in public in 1916, led by Rosa Luxemburg, Clara Zetkin, Franz Mehring, Leo Jogiches and others, building out of the *Internationale* group of socialists who had opposed the war in 1914. The Spartakusbund initially worked inside the Social Democratic Party, then inside the Independent Social Democratic Party until December 1918 when it became the Communist Party of Germany (Spartakist). After the German Revolution had begun in November 1918, which abolished the German monarchy, in January 1919 the Spartakists made an attempt at an uprising in Berlin, which was bloodily repressed by the Freikorps under the authority of the new Social Democrat government. The two Spartakist leaders, Rosa Luxemburg and Karl Liebknecht, were murdered, though their heroic courage and internationalist principles had redeemed the honour of the working class movement and ensured the name Spartacus would now forever not only live on, but be intertwined with the revolutionary socialist tradition.[12] As Liebknecht put it in his very last article, written hours before his murder, 'Spartacus – that means: fire and spirit, it means: soul and heart, it means: the will and act of the proletarian revolution. And Spartacus – that means all the hardships and yearning for happiness, all the fighting resolve of the class-conscious proletariat. Because Spartacus – that means: Socialism and World Revolution.'[13]

In 1933, the Scottish socialist novelist James Leslie

---

12 See Chris Harman, *The Lost Revolution: Germany 1918-1923* (London: Bookmarks, 1998) for full details.

13 Karl Liebknecht, 'In spite of everything!', *Die Rote Fahne*, 15 January 1919, https://www.marxists.org/archive/liebknecht-k/works/1919/01/inspite.html

Mitchell – better known under the name Lewis Grassic Gibbon for his classic literary trilogy known as *A Scots Quair* (1932-34) – published his spellbinding historical novel *Spartacus*. William Malcolm notes the historical research undertaken by Mitchell (and his wife Rebecca) in the British Museum, but 'the realistic qualities of *Spartacus* are balanced by highly romantic properties,' which link the work with Mitchell's earlier novels.[14] Mitchell did not shy away from scenes of cruel violence, or showing the depths of barbarism to which the slave-owning master-class were prepared to descend in order to crush the revolt, shaped perhaps by his own witnessing the brutality of British imperialism in the Middle East in the face of Arab nationalist movements during the 1920s while serving in the Royal Army Service Corps. As a Marxist, whose sympathies for the exiled former leading figure of the Russian Revolution, Leon Trotsky, kept him out of the Communist Party, Mitchell told the story from the point of view of the enslaved in all their multi-ethnic and multicultural diversity as opposed to 'the Masters'. Spartacus for Mitchell stood for the liberation of all: 'I know nothing of the histories or plans of men, but they'll never be peace or the State unshaken, with women suckling their children at peace and men at work in the fields with quiet hearts, but that slave and master alike is unknown in the land ... if ever we build our slave state, there'll be no slaves in it at all ... it is only the slaves themselves that can do that'.[15]

The rise of fascism in the inter-war period meant a

---

[14] William K. Malcolm, *A blasphemer and a reformer: a study of James Leslie Mitchell* (Lewis Grassic Gibbon) (Aberdeen: Aberdeen University Press, 1984), 101, 116-117. See also Hall and Stead, *A People's History of the Classics*, 248-249.

[15] Lewis Grassic Gibbon, *Spartacus* (London: Redwords, 1996), 194. This certainly has a degree of Romanticism to it, as in reality while Spartacus was certainly committed to egalitarianism, for example dividing spoils of plunder among his army equally, it seems very unlikely his programme was one of a full end to slavery. See Aldo Schiavone, *Spartacus* (Cambridge, Massachusetts: Harvard University Press, 2013), 59, 117-118.

new glorification of the authoritarian Roman Empire, indeed the name fascism came from the *fasces* [bundles of rods tied together] carried by the Roman *lictors* [bodyguards of the magistrates in the Roman Republic]. In Fascist Italy Mussolini organized new archeological excavations to explore and exploit the heritage of ancient Rome for political purposes. In response to the rise of fascist dictatorships across Europe, the Hungarian-born Jewish writer and former Communist Arthur Koestler defiantly published his first novel, *The Gladiators* (1939). Koestler's novel was however a more pessimistic reflection on the Spartacus revolt, reflecting his own growing disillusionment with the ideals of socialism amid the rise of Stalinism. As the English Marxist historian F. A. Ridley commented in his useful 1944 historical study of *Spartacus*, if Mitchell's *Spartacus* was 'a dramatically powerful narrative of imaginative reconstruction', then Koestler's *The Gladiators* was 'a less poignant but admirably detailed reconstruction of its rising against its contemporary background'.[16]

Perhaps the most famous novel, however, was that by another former Communist, the American writer Howard Fast, whose bestselling *Spartacus* was published in 1951. Fast wrote the novel after serving a three-month jail term under McCarthyism in 1950 for refusing to join in with the witch-hunt underway, and had to self-publish it initially. Fast then worked with Stanley Kubrick (and a team of other writers including the blacklisted Communist Dalton Trumbo) to help make the classic 1960 Hollywood epic film *Spartacus* starring Kirk Douglas.[17] Fast's novel

---

16 Ridley, *Spartacus*, 10. Ridley's work was 'dedicated to the immortal memory of Rosa Luxemburg, Karl Liebknecht, and the German Spartakists of 1919'. George Orwell has a useful discussion of the weaknesses of *The Gladiators* as a novel in his 1944 essay on Arthur Koestler.

17 For more discussion of the film see Phil Butland, 'Sixty Years of Spartacus', *International Socialism*, 172 (2021), https://isj.org.uk/spartacus/ For a short but interesting 2000 interview with Howard Fast about Spartacus, see here https://www.trussel.com/hf/ancient.htm Gore Vidal also worked on the script for the film Spartacus, helping ensure there was

may have played fast and lose with some of the known historical facts, as did the film, but nonetheless both the novel and the film still powerfully illuminated some of the broader truths about the oppressive nature of the Roman ruling class and the heroism of the revolt against it. For example, in one passage in Fast's novel, Marcus Licinius Crassus, the corrupt millionaire Roman general and politician who finally put down Spartacus's revolt, is imagined as later reflecting on how, after crushing what was called the 'third servile war', his soldiers rightly smashed the monuments carved out of volcanic rock on the eastern slope of Mount Vesuvius made by Spartacus's army.

> I was a soldier and I carried out the orders of the Senate. You will hear it said that the Servile War was a small thing. It's quite natural that such a view should be taken, since it profits Rome little to tell the world what a job we had with some slaves. But here, on this pleasant terrace at the home of my dear and good friend, Antonius Caius, with the company we have, we can dispense with legends. No one ever came as close to destroying Rome as Spartacus did. No one ever wounded her so terribly ... if the tokens of punishment are unpleasant, think of how I felt when I saw the ground carpeted with the bodies of the finest troops in Rome. So I didn't shrink from destroying some rock carving that the slaves had made. Quite to the contrary, I took a certain satisfaction in it. We destroyed the images most thoroughly and ground them into rubble – so that no trace of it remains. So did we destroy Spartacus and his army. So will we in time – and necessarily – destroy the very memory of what he did and how he did it. I am a fairly simple man and not particularly clever, but I know this. The order of things is that some must rule and some must serve. So the gods

---

a homoerotic subplot within the film, which can be clearly seen on the full unedited version of the film.

ordained it. So it will be.[18]

So successful in many ways were the Roman ruling class in wiping out the memory of Spartacus that the historical sources we have about him are extremely limited, and many of those we have were written by those whose sympathies lay with the Roman rulers rather than those they ruled, so have to be 'read against the grain'. As Barry Strauss notes in his valuable 2009 work, *The Spartacus War*,

> Spartacus left no writings. His followers scratched out no manuscripts. Surviving ancient narratives come from Roman or Greek writers who wrote from the point of view of the victors. To make matters worse, few of their writings survive ... Plutarch (c. AD 40s-120s) and Appian (c. AD 90s-160s) provide the most complete accounts of Spartacus to survive from antiquity but they are short, late (150-200 years after the revolt) ... even shorter is the discussion by Florus (c AD 100-150), but his concise remarks are full of significance. These three writers relied on important but now mostly lost earlier works by Sallust (86-35BC) and Livy (59BC-AD12)...[19]

Yet the Spartacus revolt itself could never be completely erased from history in the way the Roman ruling class would have liked, for it was on such a scale and lasted such a length of time as to make this impossible. As Strauss notes, 'what began as a prison breakout by

---

18 Howard Fast, *Spartacus* (London: Panther, 1970), 153. The first two 'servile wars' or slave uprisings had been in Sicily in 138-132 BCE and then again in Sicily in 104-101 BCE. On these, see Schiavone, *Spartacus*, 70-78.

19 Barry Strauss, *The Spartacus War* (London: Phoenix, 2010), 4. The accounts by Plutarch, Appian and Florus are available in translation online. See Plutarch of Chaeronea (46-c.122), *Life of Crassus*, 8-11, online at https://www.livius.org/sources/content/plutarch/plutarchs-crassus/plutarch-on-spartacus/; see Appian of Alexandria (c.95-c.165), *Civil Wars*, 1.116-120, online at https://www.livius.org/sources/content/appian/appian-spartacus/; Publius Annius Florus (c.70? – c.140?), Epitome, 2.8.3-14, online at https://www.livius.org/sources/content/florus/florus-on-spartacus/

seventy-four men armed only with cleavers and skewers had turned into a revolt by thousands' and within a year would involve something like 60,000 rebel troops, almost one in twenty of the entire enslaved population in Italy (some 1-1.5 million strong), an 'enormous army' that 'had come within a week's march of Rome itself'.

Spartacus's was antiquity's most famous slave revolt and arguably its largest. It was a revolt that absorbed southern Italy, caught Rome with its homeland virtually defenceless, led to nine defeats of Roman armies and kept antiquity's greatest military power at bay for two years.[20]

It was not until the Enlightenment and the period Eric Hobsbawm called 'the age of revolution' got underway in the eighteenth century that Spartacus as a historical figure began to take on new resonance, as we can see from the Voltaire quote with which we began. Yet that age of revolution coincided with a great age of European empire-building, linked to the breakthrough of the new capitalist world system, and along with this went a new found respect among our rulers for the 'great' generals who had built the Roman Empire. As Angus Calder once noted, in Europe 'educated men knew about Ancient Rome and were not embarrassed by any scientific understanding of history. The exploits of Caesar, they fancied, were of a kind which they themselves could

---

20 Strauss, *The Spartacus War*, 2-3. Part of the reason for the longevity and impact of the Spartacus revolt came from the way in which it took on the character of an emerging 'anti-Roman' civil war which tapped into the legacy of the previous 'Social War' led by Sulla and the wider general discontent of the Plebians, with Spartacus representing a 'new Hannibal'. However, its roots and origins as a slave revolt seem to have ultimately tragically proved an insuperable barrier to the forging of the necessary unity to have toppled the existing Roman system due to the existing ideological prejudice against slaves by the 'free' population. See Schiavone, *Spartacus*, 96, 106-107, 118. Mary Beard's recent 'popular 'history of ancient Rome, a work which downplays the importance of slavery to the system, also touches on this briefly. See Mary Beard, *SPQR: A History of Ancient Rome* (London: Profile, 2016), 248-250.

repeat.'[21] By the time European empire-building was at its height in the late nineteenth and early twentieth century, British imperialist overlords were often described as 'proconsuls' presiding over a *Pax Britannica* akin to the *Pax Romana*, Rudyard Kipling in stories such as *Regulus* glorified the British Empire as the modern Imperium Romanum, while the imperialist Jan Smuts thought that just 'as the Roman ideas guided European civilization for almost two thousand years, so the newer ideas embedded in the British constitutional and Colonial system may, when carried to their full development, guide the future civilization for ages to come'.[22]

Given our rulers today in an age of permanent inter-imperialist war still glorify Roman 'civilization', and pursue the Roman strategy of 'divide et impera' – divide and conquer – it is timely to remember the phrase of the Roman historian Tacitus in the second century CE, referring to Roman power in Britain: 'They create desolation and call it peace'.[23] It is also timely to remember the greatest ever challenge to the Roman Empire from below, that led by Spartacus, a former auxiliary drafted to fight for the Romans, who deserted,

---

21 Angus Calder, *Revolutionary Empire: The Rise of the English-Speaking Empires from the Fifteenth Century to the 1780s* (New York: E.P. Dutton, 1981), 9-10. This is not to say there is nothing to be learnt from ancient writers and historians – Marx for example thought their writings remained 'ever new'. See Prawer, *Karl Marx and World Literature*, 211.

22 Caroline Elkins, *Legacy of Violence: A History of the British Empire* (London: Bodley Head, 2022), 75-76, 123. As Chris Harman once noted in an interview in 2008, 'People who talk of our supposed "Graeco-Roman" or "Judeo-Christian" heritage ignore the fact that the wisdom of the ancient world had to be fostered in Baghdad before being passed back to Europe via Islamic Spain.' Chris Harman, 'Socialists and history: a battle for the past', *Socialist Worker*, 10 May 2008, online at https://www.marxists.org/archive/harman/2008/05/history.htm

23 Beard, *SPQR*, 18. As Steve Roskams has noted of the Western imperialist interventions of the oil-rich 'Middle East' in recent decades, 'this militarised process was portrayed in many media (without a hint of irony, it should be noted) as bringing civilisation to a region, Mesopotamia, which in fact witnessed the emergence of some of the earliest urbanised societies known to us'. Steve Roskams, 'Marx, Marxism and Classical Antiquity' in I Milevski (ed.), *Marxist Archaeology Today* (Leiden/Boston: Brill, 2024), 173.

was then captured, enslaved, and condemned to become a gladiator, before leading his break out from the gladiator barracks at Capua, 130 miles along the Appian Way from Rome. For the Roman ruling class, the bloody gladiatorial spectacles were not just a form of entertainment, 'bread and circuses', but ideologically about reinforcing the glorification of militarism and the centrality of war within Roman society. For gladiators to then not only revolt and strike out for freedom but then come so close to bringing this whole imperialist set up crashing down was particularly painful for the Roman ruling class.

Chris Harman (1942-2009), a leading member of the Socialist Workers' Party (SWP) and its forerunner organizations in Britain for many decades from the early 1960s, referred to Spartacus and his revolt amid the revolutionary year of 1968 in 'A Revolutionary Socialist Manifesto', written for the International Socialists in June 1968.[24] Chris wrote extensively about Rosa Luxemburg, Karl Liebknecht and the Spartakist League in his 1982 classic work on the German Revolution, *The Lost Revolution: Germany, 1918-1923*.[25] During the 1990s, Chris was working on his magisterial *A People's History of the World* (1999), and the year before this work was published, he gave a talk on Spartacus at Marxism festival in London in 1998. This talk – published in this volume for the first time with Chris's original speaking notes included as footnotes – provides not only a vivid account of one of the most tragic but heroic class struggles in world history, but also a fascinating historical and materialist discussion on the interrelationship between slavery, the impoverishment of the Roman peasant, and the rise and fall of the Roman Empire.[26]

---

24 This was unpublished at the time, but is now available online. See Chris Harman, '*A Revolutionary Socialist Manifesto*', https://www.marxists.org/archive/harman/1968/06/manifesto.html

25 For more on Chris Harman himself, see Alex Callinicos's 2009 obituary in *Socialist Worker*, online at https://www.marxists.org/archive/harman/obits/callinicos.htm and Chris Harman, *Selected Writings* (London: Bookmarks, 2010).

26 Harman's defence of the idea of seeing the Spartacus revolt through

Chris here of course built on Marx, whose study of ancient writers had helped him philosophically to develop his core analytical tool, the 'mode of production', embodying an internally structurally contradictory totality focused around relations of exploitation – the appropriation of part of the product of the labour of others – and the arising class struggles.[27] The idea of a 'slave mode of production' that was distinct to the classic or ancient world system was developed empirically in enormous detail by the Marxist historian Geoffrey de Ste Croix, in *The Class Struggle in the Ancient Greek World* (1981) – a classic work which as its title suggests was also concerned with subjective struggles as well as objective structures – and which also shaped Chris's analysis.[28] Later works by Marxist historians such as Chris Wickham in *Framing in the Early Middle Ages* (2005) have added new detail to our understanding of the specific forms of exploitation which emerged amid the decline and fall of the Roman Empire.[29] Such a framework – the 'slave

---

the lens of class struggle stands out against much otherwise valuable recent scholarship, for example that by Aldo Schiavone, for whom 'class struggle' is just a phenomenon in the modern world. See Schiavone, *Spartacus*, 98. For further discussion of Spartacus and the Roman Empire by Chris Harman, see *A People's History of the World* (London: Bookmarks, 1999), 71-86. For a recent scholarly overview of slavery and the Roman empire, see Brent D. Shaw, 'The Great Transformation: Slavery and the Free Republic' in Harriet I. Flower, *The Cambridge Companion to the Roman Republic* (Cambridge: Cambridge University Press, 2014), 187-212.

27 For more discussion of Marx's concept, see Chris Harman, 'Base and Superstructure' in Chris Harman *Marxism and History* (London: Bookmarks, 1998) and also Alex Callinicos, *Making History* (London: Polity, 1987), 41-52.

28 G.E.M. de Ste Croix, *The Class Struggle in the Ancient Greek World* (London: Duckworth, 1981), 52. For more on de Ste Croix's contribution, see Paul Blackledge, *Reflections on the Marxist Theory of History* (Manchester: Manchester University Press, 2006), 103-110, while for an excellent recent discussion, see Steve Roskams, 'Marx, Marxism and Classical Antiquity'.

29 See Chris Harman, 'Shedding new light on the Dark Ages: A review of Chris Wickham, Framing the Early Middle Ages: Europe and the Mediterranean, 400-800, *International Socialism*, 109 (2006). https://isj.org.uk/shedding-new-light-on-the-dark-ages/

mode of production' – showed the limitations to the potentialities of any such slave revolt such as that of Spartacus amid the scarcity of the pre-capitalist world, and helps explain why Spartacus's rebel slave army could only really imagine liberation by fleeing away from the centre of the Roman Empire, and trying to recreate an earlier more egalitarian society outside of the system. It is only since the huge productive forces unleashed by modern capitalism that the potential to transcend not only scarcity but class society itself once and for all has existed in human history. It is only through the working class taking democratic collective control of those productive forces through class struggle and socialist revolution that the potential of such a new society, one without any exploitation or oppression, can finally become a reality. For that, the millions of people globally who are inspired and moved by the sentiment 'I'm Spartacus!' in Kubrick's film need to get organised. The Palestinian Marxist Tony Cliff, founder of the SWP, ended his autobiography, *A World to Win*, with words with which it seems fitting to close:

> Cato the Elder, a member of the Roman Senate, used to end all his speeches with the following words: 'Cartago delenda est' – Carthage must be destroyed. And finally Rome did destroy Carthage. We have to end with these words, 'The revolutionary party must be built.'[30]

---

30 Tony Cliff, *A World to Win: Life of a Revolutionary* (London: Bookmarks, 2000), 234.

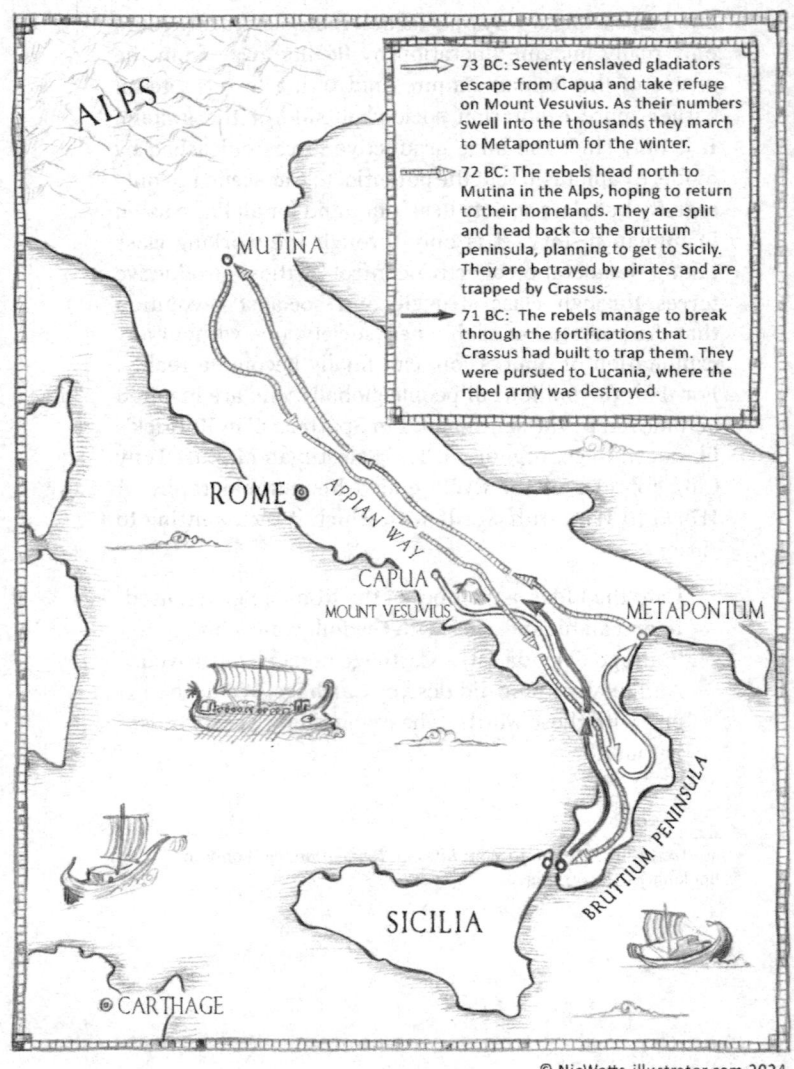

SPARTACUS / CHRIS HARMAN

THE REASON WE ARE TALKING about Spartacus is for two reasons. One is that the history of the class struggle in the Roman Empire, I find, is of enormous interest, enormously fascinating at a time when we are told that the class struggle is finished, that it's out of date, ideology is finished, and so forth, it's worth understanding the extent to which every phase in human history for the last five thousand years has been characterised by, and dominated by, class struggle.

There is also another reason, which is that Spartacus is one of those figures who, when you become a socialist, you hear about him, you hear about the slave revolt, it is something you automatically identify with. Karl Marx and the Marx family used to play a game, I think, on Sundays and at Christmas, which is a bit like one of those silly things they have in the *Guardian*, you know, where they do a figure and you have to write through what your favourite things are. And so the Marx family set down this list. And Marx was asked, 'what is your favourite character from history?' And Karl Marx had no hesitation whatsoever in saying 'Spartacus', the slave who rose up against the oppressors and challenged the might of the Roman Empire. Rosa Luxemburg, in the horror of the First World War, when she had to have a name for her organisation, called it the Spartakusbund, the Spartacus League, identifying with Spartacus.

It's not surprising that one of the best films made

in the grim period when Hollywood was controlled by McCarthyism, one of the few films to break through that, was the film starring Kirk Douglas as Spartacus, which gives some feeling for this great revolt.

There's two excellent novels on Spartacus, one by Lewis Grassic Gibbon, the great Scottish novelist. I think it's the only one of his novels that I've read which compares with *A Scots Quair*, and the other of which by the American left-wing writer of the 1930s Howard Fast. There is a ballet by Khachaturian, the Russian composer, a ballet, *Spartacus*. And therefore the name has a resonance.

Now, unfortunately, to move from the resonance of what we know about the heroism of Spartacus to actually what was involved in the revolt, there's very sparse information. Indeed, it could even be said that one reason I volunteered to do this meeting was knowing that it's only five pages you have to read to understand everything which is known about the historic Spartacus, three pages from Plutarch and two pages from Appian. It should be added, these were not written at the time of the Spartacus revolt, they were written, I think, 100, 200 years later. Clearly, at that time, because there's no printing, books would be written in just three or four copies, they disappeared, it may well be that at some earlier stage they read earlier writings which gave much more detail. And the two accounts differ in a whole number of respects from each other. But what emerges is this.

The Spartacus Revolt

Spartacus was a war captor of the Romans, who was enslaved, and with the other war captors was put in as a gladiator to perform in what I think was one of the great horrors of the Roman system, the fights where gladiators fought to death in front of spectators. Against this situation, between 74-73 BCE, a group of these gladiators got together, seventy-odd of them. They decided better to fight than to just suffer this humiliating death, rose up, broke out of the gladiator camp, and established themselves. They then set up, and it's not clear in the sources, but clearly, they somehow overpowered other Romans, began to gather around them a wider number of people, and then began to appear as some sort of force, threatening one local bit of the empire which the Roman Republic had established in Italy.

At that point, and it's quite interesting what's said here, the reaction of Romans was just to laugh at this. The Roman ruling class, and I'll come to this later, already ruling all of Italy, parts of Spain, parts of France, what's called Gaul, parts of Greece, and so on and so forth, and having conquered the great counter-power to Rome, Carthage, laughed at this small band of gladiators. As Appian writes, 'at the beginning, the revolt had been laughed at and regarded as trivial because it was against gladiators'. The Romans found it difficult to find any generals prepared to go and fight these gladiators, not because they were frightened at first that the gladiators would beat them, but they thought 'We are the great Romans, we're the great heroes...why should we go and fight them?'

Nevertheless, the Romans eventually got together an army, thought they were going for an easy kill, surrounded the gladiators on the hill [Mount Vesuvius], this is according to Plutarch's account, they surround the gladiators on the hill, blocked off every path, and thought all they had to do was walk slowly up the hill and butcher the gladiators. The Romans had two or three hundred years of experience of military techniques, which seemed capable of beating any other army in the Mediterranean world, the known world at the time. The gladiators had experience fighting other gladiators in the ring, some had experience of fighting the Romans before they were captured. They also had ingenuity. While the Romans are marching up the hill, the gladiators, there were sorts of vines hanging down from various trees down the hill. While the Romans were marching up the hill, intent upon killing every single gladiator, the gladiators climbed down the vines, got behind the Romans, and inflicted a defeat upon the Roman forces.

At that point, then it becomes clear that groups of other slaves from across Italy began leaving their masters to join the gladiators. The reports are that some shepherds and some herders from the hills, a poor Roman population who were driven to marginal existence by the Roman system, which I will come back to later, join the gladiators. The Spartacus army became quite big. At this point, the Romans began to send more serious forces against the gladiators. The Spartacus army beat the Roman forces, but it still wasn't powerful enough to dream of conquering all of Italy as a whole.

At this point, there seems to have been some sort of dispute inside the Spartacus army about which way to follow. One position was, 'look, there's all this wealth in Rome around us, all this wealth of Italy, let's just seize some of the wealth, establish ourselves, somehow have a good time'. The other position, which seems to be the position Spartacus himself put, was 'we're too weak to defeat the Roman Empire. What we can do is march out of the Roman Empire essentially. We march up across the Alps which separate Italy from Gaul, march into Gaul, much of which hadn't yet been conquered by the Romans, once we're in Gaul, we're in a situation then in which we can find ways to get back to the countries from which we were initially kidnapped'.

They marched up towards the Alps, but for some reason when they reached the Alps, they decided not to cross the Alps, probably because they were frightened they may be hit by a Roman army coming from behind, whereupon they reversed... now, I'm assuming here everyone has some knowledge of the geography of Italy. If you don't, you just have to imagine a great big boot, a woman's boot.... So you march to the top of the boot, where you are faced with the Alpine passes, they then reversed around, marched back southwards.

At this point, the Roman ruling class began to take the revolt slightly more seriously than they had in the past, and the Roman ruling class sent armies under a couple of consuls. The consuls were the officials elected by the Roman ruling class each year, key figures of the Roman ruling class, very, very prestigious. These were serious armies. This was not some small force sent to deal with a small group of malcontents. These were serious forces.

In battles outside Rome, the Spartacus army beat the picked army of the Roman ruling class. Indeed, if you are to believe some interpretations of what happened, this is the interpretation put forward in Grassic Gibbons' novel, Rome itself was a city which if the slave army wanted to, the slave army could have taken Rome. The slave army decided not to, and we can perhaps come to some discussion on why not afterwards. Instead, the slave army, after hesitating around Rome, marched right down to the toe of Italy. Again, Spartacus's intention seems to have been to escape from Italy. Appian and Plutarch say that he thought he had some agreement with the pirates who controlled the straits between Italy and Sicily, that they would provide him with boats, the slave army would disembark from Italy, escape to Sicily, North Africa, or perhaps to Syria, where many of them come from, and in that way, achieve their freedom. 'Never put your faith or trust in crooks and gangsters', which I think is a good saying. I remember Brendan Behan halfway through his experiences in prison made the point that most gangsters vote Tory. But the reality is that when they got to the toe of Italy, they found the boats weren't there to disembark them.

At this point, the Romans sent serious forces against them. A man called Crassus and a man called Pompey, who later became one of the three people along with Caesar who briefly controlled Rome before he's disposed of by Caesar, moved serious armies in. They tried to trap the slave army on the toe of Italy. And this is not a marginal thing by the Romans. It involved the Roman army, the legions, physically building a huge ditch to cut off the toe of Italy from the rest of Italy, to keep the Spartacus army trapped in the toe of Italy. It's very well imagined what could have happened in Grassic Gibbon's book because you have this army, stuck there through the winter, conditions deteriorating. It looks as if the slave army is going to be absolutely smashed, and then through a fantastic bit of military ingenuity, the slave army break out, break across the ditch, break through the Romans' lines, and then begin to march back up towards Rome.

At which point, serious forces, your're now talking about the whole force established by the Roman Republic, are being used against them. Pompey, Crassus, come in, serious forces used. First serious battle, the slave army has some success, but the slave army splits up after some row between the leaders. The second, the last battle, the slave army is defeated but fighting fantastically courageously. There's no doubt the last battle was a serious battle. It was a battle in which the slaves inflicted serious damage on the Romans. The slaves suffered a huge level of defeat, and 6,000 of the slaves were then taken and crucified along the road leading south from Rome.

Now, in this, it should be said, one thing in the film, which is probably wrong, is that Spartacus himself wasn't crucified. You have two accounts of what happened, one account is that he just died in the battle, the other account, I think it is in Plutarch, describes Spartacus injured, fighting at the last, trying to fight his way through the Roman army to get to the Roman general, to kill the Roman general. That's his last act and he's cut down at the height of the battle.[1]

Class structure and slavery in the Roman Republic

Now, that's the basic bare bones of what happened. Why is it important? Well, one of reasons it is important of course is that Rome at the time Spartacus rebelled, Rome was

---

[1] Details from A Lintott, 'Political history', in J A Crook, A Lintott and E Rawson (eds.) *Cambridge Ancient History*, vol. IX, (Cambridge, 1986), 221-223.

beginning to become what we would call today a hegemonic power, a power dominating the Mediterranean. In the thirty or forty years after the defeat of the slave army, Rome moved from being an Italian power with some possessions in North Africa and Greece and Spain, to dominating and conquering the whole of the Mediterranean basin, establishing this huge empire of fifty or sixty million people.

Now, to understand the background of this you need to understand a few things about the Roman Empire itself. The first thing to understand is the Roman Empire was an empire which began with this relatively small town on the Tiber, which grew, basically because it succeeded. The Romans, having thrown off the Etruscans, the alleged date was 509 BCE. The Etruscans were a more advanced people, in the center of Italy, who controlled the Romans and had the Romans in tribute, until about 509 BCE. The Romans rebelled against the Etruscans, and then succeeded in establishing an army which was capable of dominating the neighboring Italian towns and Italian areas.

As they dominated these areas, the Romans established a system whereby each town they conquered, they forced that town to pay money to Rome. Therefore, the Roman ruling class became richer and richer and richer by exploiting the other towns around it. Some of the towns became what were called allies of Rome. That is their population received certain sorts of citizen rights of Rome, certain rights, others were just tributaries who had to pay funds.

On this basis, the Romans built a peasant army. What essentially the Romans discovered is an army of peasants, hardworking people used to working in and out, night and day, year after year after year, could be built up into a force, which is both a military force, but along with the military force, would also carry out engineering projects along the way. What I mean is build their own roads, build their own camps, establish fortifications, barricades, a fighting force which the Roman soldiers are described as carrying not merely his weapons, but also carrying trenching tools, spades, cooking pots, the whole paraphernalia, described as being partly a fighter, partly a mule. These armies of the Roman legions, moving around, conquering people by this immense power, based upon a peasant army.

But from the beginning of the Roman Republic, the peasant army did the fighting, the people who benefited from the fighting were a very small group of ruling class families. Early on in the history of the Roman Republic, you have the famous conflicts between the Patricians and the Plebeians. If people have read *The Communist Manifesto* they may remember Karl Marx's remark, 'the history of all hitherto existing society is the history of class struggle...patrician and plebian...'. This struggle essentially involved a fight between two separate groups of citizens of Rome. The old families who had established their control upon the wealth coming in from the newly conquered territories, and the population of Rome, who were discriminated against and not allowed that control. A description of the way in which the Patricians treated the Plebians is from a Roman historian called Sallust. And again, he's writing some hundreds of years after the event, I think five hundred years after the event. But he describes how the Patricians treat the people as slaves, make decisions concerning the execution of flogging, throw them into the land, crush them by cruel practices, loaded them with debt, forced them to fight in the army, and so on and so forth.[2]

Only fifteen years after the republic was founded and the Etruscans were driven out, you have the first rebellion of the Plebians against the Patricians. Interestingly, it takes the form of a sort of strike. Again, there's various reports of what happened, but it seems that what happened is the Plebeians were told by the Patricians that

---

2 'The Patricians treated the people as slaves, made decisions concerning their execution and flogging, drove them from their lands. Crushed them by these cruel practices and above all by the load of debt occasioned by the necessity to contribute both money and military service for continual wars, the common people, armed took up position on Mons Sacer and on the Aventine and acquired for themselves tribunes of the people and some legal rights.' Sallust, *The Histories*, vol 1, (Oxford 1992), 24.

you've got to come to the army and come and fight one of our battles. The Plebeians marched out of the city, armed, sat down with their arms and said, 'we're not fighting until you concede our demands'. This process was called 'secession' – imagine the working class seceding from capitalist society – this process of secession took place several times over the next couple of hundred years. Each stage, the Plebeians forcing the Patricians to concede certain rights. At the end of that period of 200 years, the form of distinction between Plebians and Patricians didn't exist anymore. Unfortunately the mass of the Roman peasantry gained very little from this.[3] What happened was that a small layer of the Plebeians were allowed to join the Patrician elite, get jobs in the Roman government, participate in the wealth coming from the Empire, the mass of Plebeians were actually left at the bottom of society in the same precarious situation.[4]

And therefore, you have this first wave of battle,

---

[3] The tribunes would 'provide such protection by literally stepping between them and their intended victims', knowing that the Plebians had sworn a collective oath to lynch any magistrate who touched a tribune. At first they 'stood to the official state magistrates almost as shop stewards to company directors'. But eventually they became an integral part of the constitution, obtaining the power to arrest and imprison state officials. And the last great struggle in 287, provoked by the scale of debt burden on about half the Roman population, brought to an end the formal powers of the Patricians, opening all offices up to Plebeians. See P A Brunt, *Social Conflicts in the Roman Republic* (London, 1971), 51, 87; G.E.M. de Ste Croix, *The Class Struggle in the Ancient Greek World* (London, 1983), 334-335.

[4] The victories of the Plebeians still did not bring about an Athens-type democracy. For, not for the last time in history, the interests of those who led the Plebian struggles were not the same as the mass of those taking part. The Plebeians, it is important to add, were not an economic class, but a mass made up of all those who were denied the hereditary political rights of the Patrician families. This mass clearly included all the poor and all the small landowners. But it also included some people who had grown rich as the republic expanded but who were still discriminated against politically. Such people had much greater resources and time to engage in political affairs than the average small farmer or craftsman, and tended to dominate the Plebian assemblies. For them the struggle was over in 287 when they gained equal rights with the Patricians, while for the mass of people the disparities in wealth were still growing greater than ever.

Patricians versus Plebeians. It was praised later by many Roman historians showing 'we showed our moderation. This isn't like these Greeks who go murder each other in civil wars in the cities. The patricians and the plebians had this row but it came to this peaceful solution with a constitutional framework'.[5] You can imagine a Tony Blair describing it, a 'Tonius Blairus' describing it. But actually, the fundamental reality was the Roman Empire remained a class structure, and the class structure showed itself again as the Roman Empire expanded. Between the 4th and the 3rd centuries, the Romans were involved in in a war for life and death against the other empire trying to expand to the Mediterranean basin, the city of Carthage, just the other side of the Mediterranean, in North Africa. During the period of the wars against Carthage, the class struggle in Rome itself seemed to disappear. I don't believe the peasants were any happier, the conditions any better, and so on and so forth. Once the war against Carthage was finished, the antagonism between the mass of the Roman peasantry and the Roman ruling class came to the fore with enormous momentum.

Essentially, what happened was the victory of the Roman armies led to two sorts of immense wealth flooding to Rome. One was the immense wealth coming from the territories which were conquered by Rome. The territories which were conquered were forced to pay tribute to Rome. Tribute meant if you were a North African city conquered by Rome, a fifth or a third of the wealth you produced had to be basically put into boats and sent to Rome, as well as all the pillaging of the cities,

---

[5] As Brunt points out, Roman writers like Dionysus and Halicarnassus were to praise the 'moderation shown in the struggle of the orders, which contrasted with the revolutionary bloodshed familiar to Greek cities. But what had been achieved? In form a greater measure of democratic control. That was to prove an illusion. Plebians had been admitted to office. But by giving up their monopoly, the Patricians perpetuated for themselves a share of power. A new nobility arose to which only a few Plebians were admitted, and which was as dominant as the Patricians had been...The old social conflicts were to reappear, but it was harder for the poor to find champions once the political aspirations of the rich Plebians had been satisfied.' Brunt, *Social Conflicts*, 58.

the gold, the silver, and so forth, the systematic pillaging of the empire by Rome.[6]

The second form of wealth which went parallel with this pillaging, was the massive enslavement of populations. You know, anyone who believes, you know, there was myth about 'the glory that was Rome', the wonders of the Roman Empire, 'Roman civilization'. You know, it's quite normal when the Romans conquered a city, to kill the whole male population, you enslave all of the women and children, and you deport them to Rome. Or if they don't put up so much resistance, you don't kill the whole male population, you kill 1 in 5 or 1 in 10 of the male population, you enslave the others. So for instance when the Romans won a war against the Macedonians the calculation is 150,000 people transferred from Macedonia to the slave markets.[7] Then, of course, you had this process operating whereby the Roman rich got the benefits of the tribute. They got the wealth from the looting. I mean, one description is I think of Pompey who was regarded as generous to his troops, because when they looted the city, he took half the money and he divided the rest of the money among the 30,000 or 40,000 troops equally, so a '50/50 partnership'...

The Roman rich had these vast sums of wealth. The vast sums of wealth then enabled them to buy the slaves off the Roman state, and they systematically then established a situation in which they began tilling their estates with slaves.[8] And their calculation was quite

---

[6] Some of the poorer peasants were settled in the new territory, relieving their plight for a period. But by far the major gainers from conquest were the rich. They were not only able to expand their landholdings, but also received vast amounts of other sorts of wealth. 'Very large sums flowed into private hands in Italy from abroad ... The great bulk went to men of the upper and middle classes...' Much of the loot went on luxury consumption, but some went further expanding the landholding of the rich, raising the price of land and encouraging moneylenders to dispossess indebted peasants. See A.H.M. Jones, *The Roman Economy* (London 1974), 116.

[7] Jones, *The Roman Economy*, 122.

[8] Big landowners could buy slaves very cheaply and use them to cultivate their big 'latifundia' estates at low cost: 'Cato's slaves received a tunic

simply this. 'The Roman army is invincible. Every year, we conquer more people. Every time we conquer more people, we enslave more people, there's an endless supply of slaves.'

Along with that went another calculation. If you have got a peasant tilling the land, you have to worry about what happens to the peasant in thirty years' time. Peasants don't live that long. The only way you can guarantee having a peasant in thirty years' time, is if the peasant has a family and the family have children. That is you not only have got to worry about the cost of upkeep of the peasant, you've got the cost of the upkeep of the peasant, of the female peasant, and of the peasant's children. And it's quite expensive. On the other hand, a slave, who cares if the slave dies in twenty years' time and you haven't replaced it, he hasn't had children and so on and so forth. All you do, the Roman army is victorious, we will have more slaves, an endless flow of money. Indeed, 'the wealth we make from land with land with slaves, we use to build a bigger army. We then use this to conquer more territory to get more slaves'. An endless process of building up, expanding the wealth of the Roman ruling class, expanding the size of the Roman Empire.

Therefore it's important to understand it was a crude calculation in terms of almost profit and loss in terms of the Roman ruling class and their attitude towards slavery. They enslaved people because they saw slaves as a means of dispensing with the need to keep alive the Roman peasantry.[9] And then you find the situation characteristically, the more successful the Roman armies were in war, the more impoverished the Roman peasants became. All the accounts which you have from the period,

---

and a blanket every year and ate no meat'. Brunt, *Social Conflicts*, 33.

9 It was much more costly to employ a landless Roman peasant, with a family to bring up. And so those who lost their land found it very difficult to get anything other than temporary, seasonable work. And the number losing their land continued to grow, as the conscription of able-bodied males into the army for years at a time made it difficult for peasant families to avoid debt.

for instance, this man, Sallust, I can read great accounts from him, page after page, describing the impoverishment of the mass of the peasantry in this period.[10] And it's important because there's always the old argument, you know, we have it in the form today, 'Do workers in the West benefit from the exploitation of the Third World? Do white American workers benefit from the oppression of black Americans?' Often behind it, people always assume where you have slavery, the free worker must benefit from the oppression of the slave, the free peasant must benefit from the fact that a slavery exists on a massive scale. The reality in the Roman Empire, the growth of slavery on the one hand, and the impoverishment of the mass of the Roman people on the other.[11]

And you can see it in the crude statistics, you find the free population of Rome declines once you have slavery on a massive scale, that is the peasants can't afford to have children, they are driven from one scale of poverty to another. Some of them end up selling themselves into slavery as the only means by which they can stay alive. Infanticide, massive scale of abortion not because the peasant women want to exercise the right to choose but because no one wanted to have children, a situation which you couldn't keep the children alive. These are the characteristic features. The free population of Italy declines as you have the spread of slavery taking place.[12]

---

10 As Sallust wrote of the early first century BCE: 'A few men controlled everything in peace and war. They disposed of the treasury, the provinces, the magistracies, honours and triumphs. The people was oppressed by military service and by want. The booty of war fell into the hands of the generals and few others. Meantime parents or little children of the soldiers were driven out of their homes by powerful neighbours'. Quoted by Brunt, *Social Conflicts*, 15.

11 A.H.M. Jones, who is said never to have read Marx, argued 'The vast import of slaves increased the destitution of the Italian peasantry.' Jones, *The Roman Economy*, 123; St Croix, Class struggle... 356. So you had growth of slavery on the one hand, impoverishment of the mass of Romans on the other, i.e. peasants did not benefit from slavery. But at the same time, ruling ideology kept peasants apart from slaves.

12 This is shown by the way in which as the Roman state grew from strength to strength, the numbers of the free population stagnated or even fell. The explanation, PA Brunt tells us: 'Must be sought partly in

For the Roman ruling class, the method became even cruder. We fight our wars with this peasant army. It's wonderful because when the peasant is not on his land, the peasant can't be producing crops. He comes back from the war. He's in debt. The people who lent him money are the Roman rich. The Roman rich buy the land, sell it to the landowners with the loot, which the peasant has got in the wars. This is the whole basis on which the Roman Empire was built and sustained. The idea of an endless supply of slaves. The slaves come in. You don't care about them reproducing. You get them, you work them to death. You replace them by more slaves. At the same time, you drive the peasantry off the land, impoverish the Roman people, and the Roman aristocracy get richer and richer and richer.

The revival of the class struggle

Now, it's against this background that you not only have Spartacus's revolt, you have another very, very bitter wave of class struggles in Rome, and then you have the establishment of the Roman Empire. Now, the class struggles in Rome itself are of immense interest because essentially, the moment the Romans have conquered Carthage, then you have the revival of the class struggle in Rome. It begins in 133 BCE. Essentially, what happens is the complex Roman constitution, you remember you've done away with the formal distinction between Plebeians and Patricians. Allegedly, all Roman citizens have the right to elect people to certain positions. In 133 BCE, the impoverished peasantry, who are citizens of the Roman state, providing they can turn up to Rome to vote in the elections, vote in as the most powerful figure, a man called

---

the high incidence of celibacy and childlessness. The poor especially could not afford to marry and, if married, to raise children. Families were limited by abortion and infanticide, if not by contraception.' He also suggests that the many children abandoned by poor parents would end up for sale in the slave markets. P A Brunt, *Italian Manpower*, 225BC-AD14 (Oxford, 1971), 9.

Tiberius Gracchus.[13]

Tiberius Gracchus is a former general. He himself is personally terrified as he can see that the slave system is undermining the military strength of the Roman Empire. He puts forth a programme really saying 'the rich are screwing the poor, the poor are suffering, this is weakening the Roman state, and so on and so forth'. He calls for redistribution of land to the poor, handing of public lands over to the poor. Public lands by and large were allegedly owned by the state, but being used by wealthy private senatorial families. On this basis, he builds up a very, very powerful position in Rome. For three years, he dominates Roman politics.[14]

The Roman ruling class at first seem to make concessions to him, but they themselves get more and more bitter and angry with him, and they seize the opportunity. The calculation is his base is the peasants, they choose a time to have the elections when the peasants are in the countryside pulling in the harvests. And at that moment, a group of senators get together and then move against him in the Senate. They say, 'this man is trying to establish a dictatorship. He's trying to turn himself into a king. We must do something about him'. He tries to organize a demonstration outside the Senate of his supporters. Basically, the rich bastards, the young, nasty, rich, charge out of the Senate, cut their way through his supporters, and kill him.[15] As simple as that. You know,

---

13 In 133 BCE, a member of one of the aristocratic families, Tiberius Gracchus, won a tribuneship. Despite his background, he was worried by the increased poverty of the mass of peasantry. His motives were partly the military security of the republic. He could see that the peasant backbone of the Roman legions was slowly being destroyed by the influx of slaves.

14 His programme was one which excited the poorer peasants and infuriated the major part of the rich senatorial class. For it involved distributing the poor large areas of public land which were being farmed by the big landowners. The rural poor flooded into Rome to back his proposal, covering the walls of the city with placards backing it and ensuring it was passed by the state's 'tribal assembly'.

15 The Senators were horrified, and did their best to block the measure, attempting to veto it and refusing to provide funds to implement it. But

ruling classes, all their talk about glory and honor and so on and so forth, when it comes to dealing with anyone, even one of their own members who actually gets up their nose, they behave exactly like this.

Ten years later, the situation is repeated almost so it's like reading a script repeated verbatim. Tiberius' brother, Gaius Gracchus, again wins an important elected position, for a couple of years is the dominating figure in Roman politics. And again, the senatorial elite, you can imagine all these rich people who write in *The Times* and *The Daily Telegraph*, saying 'this demagogue, this man is trying to establish a dictatorship, overcoming our ancient Roman rights, overcoming our freedom, and so on and so forth'. All this talk is used again to organise a body, this time a body of young men, plus 3,000 Cretan mercenaries, what people called in the French Revolution, the *jeunesse dorée*, the gilded youth, the rich upper class people with the right accents and the right background, and the right education, who together with the mercenaries, set out, cut down Gaius Gracchus, kill him basically.[16] They think they've destroyed

---

they did not restrict themselves to 'constitutional' measures. They prepared to use force as Tiberius stood for re-election as Tribune. Tiberius' support came from the country folk, but most of these had left to the city for harvesting. He could not depend upon the urban poor. These had long ago left the countryside and were not interested in resettling there. What is more, individually they were often dependent for a livelihood on favours from the rich families and could be induced to join in pro-Senate mobs. As Tiberius protested that the tribune election had been stolen from him-by fraud, the Senate met. A body of senators demanded the consul to execute Tiberius. When the consul rejected their plea, they told him he was betraying the constitution, rushed out of the building with their armed retainers, and clubbed Tiberius Gracchus and his supporters to death. Other consuls then endorsed this murder and executed more of his followers, claiming there had been a 'revolutionary conspiracy'. Details in Brunt, *Social Conflicts* and in A Lintott, 'Political History', in *Cambridge Ancient History*, vol IX, 69.

16 Ten years later, this time the champion of the poor was Tiberius' brother Gaius. He came forward with a somewhat similar programme, won enormous support from the peasants and some backing from a layer of the new rich, the equites, who were excluded from formal political power by the Senatorial elite. He was elected Tribune and was able to dominate Roman politics for the next three years, drawing more popular support as he began to distribute newly conquered lands to the poor, banned the conscription of under 18 year-olds, and subsidised grain for the city's

the class struggle in Rome. A bitter class struggle.

The two Gracchus brothers are quite interesting because on one hand, they were from the upper classes. They were from military backgrounds. They were not representatives of the peasantry in the sense that they weren't the elected representatives of that group. They were elected, but they were upper class figures who raised a political programme which could appeal to the peasantry. In their eyes, I think they saw the political programme, in so far as they understood it, as also the salvation of the Roman Republic and the Roman Empire. They were far sighted enough to see an empire based upon catching slaves in order to catch more slaves in order to catch more slaves in order to catch more slaves is an empire which eventually is going to undermine its own base, because you have to talk about what is the social base at the centre of it, what is the force at the centre holding it together. Once you've destroyed the Roman peasantry, their logic was, there's no force. The force which has made Roman armies successful in the past, which enabled the Roman senatorial elite to have such high living standards, is the Roman peasant, the Roman peasants who conquered the slaves. Once you have an empire just based upon slavery, upon slavery and slavery, you undermine the military strength of the empire. In a certain sense they had quite a far-sighted view of the central contradiction inside the Roman Empire. At the same time, they did get peasant support around it. The problem is the peasant support wasn't sufficient for them to defeat the senatorial elite.[17]

---

masses. All these measures infuriated the main body of the Senators. In 121 BE they took their revenge. While the consul Optimus stationed 3,000 Cretan troops in the city, the Senate summoned Gaius to appear before it. When he refused, the Senate voted for Optimus to 'defend the republic'. He then distributed arms to the Senate's supporters and unleashed his Cretan troops, to murder Gaius Gracchus and execute up to 3,000 of his supporters. Again accounts of what happened are to be found in Brunt, *Social Conflicts*, 83-92, and Lintott, 'Political History', 77-84.

17 The Roman poor revered the Gracchus brothers as martyrs, making daily offerings at their graves, and both Tiberius and Gaius do seem to have been motivated by genuine feelings for the sufferings of the masses. But their programme was essentially a programme of reform, aimed at

The peasantry, this leads onto a whole different discussion, but historically, these people are a class capable of overthrowing empires, rising up, smashing, but not holding on to its conquest once it's won. Because if you're a peasant, you have to go back to the land. Once you're on the land, you disperse in a very, very wide geographical area. You don't have the concentration of forces needed to hold on and to control your own leaders and maintain your own strength. Well, the result was the peasant revolt was smashed.

That wasn't the end of the class struggle. The whole period from about 110 BCE to the victory of Julius Caesar in 49 BCE was a period of repeated bitter struggles. I mean, again, I think it's Sallust who described it as riots, dissension, assassinations, murders, fighting, and so on and so forth.[18] The difficulty is, the leaders which began to emerge to represent the peasant interests if you like, were increasingly not even like the Gracchus brothers, principled people with some sort of programme, not a peasant programme but a programme which nonetheless saw the peasantry at central, but increasingly figures who you who saw that because of the sheer sharpness

---

strengthening the Roman state and enhancing its ability to exploit the rest of the empire. They seem to have half-grasped that slavery, while enriching the big landowners, was weakening the base of the Roman economy. Their answer, however, was certainly not to appeal to the slave to free themselves and restricted the role of the poor peasants that of a pressure group within the existing constitutional setup. It did not even have much to offer the urban poor of Rome itself, who remained depending on the Senatorial rich for favours. As result, the Senate had only to bide its time until the Gracchus brothers were momentarily weakened and then could dispose of them in the bloodiest manner. Brunt, *Social Conflicts*, 92. There were slave revolts – a formidable slave revolt in Sicily at time of Tiberius Gracchus – but he made no appeal to it. He saw it as threat to empire to be countered by strengthening the peasantry, not appealing to the slaves.

18 The murder of Gaius Gracchus subdued the poor. But it did not deal with their bitterness. Nor did it prevent the new rich 'equites' resenting the political hold of the old rich families through the Senate. Sallust summed up the history of Rome over the next three quarters of a century as 'frequent riots, party strife and eventually civil war … during which a few powerful men … were attempting to win powerful rule masquerading as champions of the Senate or the people …' Sallust, *The Histories*, 25.

of the class division in Rome, figures who saw they can make their own career by sort of feeding on the popular discontent, but just channeling it into their own careerism.

Even this, most of them ended up under the knives of the senatorial elite ... Marius, Saturninus, Sulpicus, Cinna...[19] All of them made their careers in this way. The last, probably the most opportunist, was a man called Catiline. He was an opportunist because he was involved in the murder of one of the previous leaders of the popular party, then he became bankrupt and tried to organise a league of all the bankrupts in the Roman Empire, and then appealed to the peasants, even appealed to some groups inside Italy who had been done down by the Romans. He tried to organise a force behind him.[20] But there was

---

19 Marius, Saturninus, Sulpicus, Cinna, all tried to advance their own careers by appealing to the poor. The rich reacted with barbarism. Saturninus was lynched when 'all the respectable elements in society appeared in arms with their retainers'. So leader of rich Sulla imposed a reign of terror on all those who had resisted him. Even the dissidents among the very rich suffered from 'proscriptions', rewards for the killing of named individuals whose land was confiscated by the state: according to one source, 40 senators and 1,600 equites suffered. But Sulla did more than restore order in the most bloody manner for the old rich. He also showed that any general with enough wealth to buy the allegiance of the ordinary soldiers could take the city for himself. It was a lesson many a subsequent general was to take to heart. See Appian, according to Brunt, *Social Conflicts*, 197.

20 In 64 BC it was the turn of a former Sulla henchman, Catiline, allegedly involved in the torture and murder of Marius's son, to try to restore his own fortunes by raising the standard of popular revolt. Indebtedness was ruining the peasantry more than ever. Sulla's own ex-soldiers wrote a letter suggesting they might even be being enslaved for debt: 'after the loss of their patrimony they were not allowed to retrain the freedom of their persons'. Catiline himself was bankrupt and was bitter after losing an election. In desperation 'he paraded in public with a motley throng of Sulla veterans and peasants' and began to plan a coup which, by promising a cancellation of debts, appealed equally to impoverished peasants and indebted nobles. The consul Cicero learnt of the coup and took immediate countermeasures, recruiting a select band of young men to protect himself and the city and arresting and executing Catiline's leading supporters. Catiline himself fled from the city to try to take the lead in a peasant rebellion which had broken out to the north of Rome in Etruria, but was killed in battle. Catiline' s was the last rebellion which was based, however hypocritically, upon a call to the poor to take up arms. See Brunt, *Social Conflicts*, 129-130.

a succession of them. The senatorial elite, sometimes make concessions, sometimes gave ground for a year or two years, but at the end of the day, organise the groups to go out and physically murder the opposition. But they established a degree of polarisation in Roman society which meant that once you had a successful general emerge, who was prepared to play on the popular discontent, but yet was powerful enough not to be killed by the senatorial elite, you had the basis of a new form of organisation in Roman society.[21] It's essentially what Julius Caesar did. Julius Caesar who had a certain reputation as being, I don't know if you'd say 'on the left', you know, 'vaguely sympathetic to some of the previous dissidents.' He conquered Gaul in the most brutal manner. People think Julius Caesar was a great man. I think it's estimated he killed one million people in his life. He conquered Gaul, marched his army into Rome, and was successful because he could play off the discontent of the mass of the population against the senatorial elite, balance between the two, and establish a new regime.[22] But of course, the new regime, unlike the sort of programme which the Gracchus brothers had put forward, the new regime which Julius Caesar established was based as much upon systematic slavery as any previous regime. Slavery in

---

21 The bitterness against the rich persisted. Indeed, it began to infect as never before the urban poor of Rome itself. Their conditions of life were atrocious and their livelihoods insecure. They lived in tenements 60 or 70 feet high, squeezed together in a density seven or eight times that of a modern western city, their homes in constant danger of collapsing or catching fire, with no water and no access to the sewers. Many could only look forward to seasonal labouring work in the docks in the summer, and faced near starvation in the winter when corn shortages raised the price. Yet the very miserableness of their condition had prevented them fighting for their own interests. They were dependent for physical survival on the bribes rich Senators would hand out to their clients, and often taken the senate's side in riots. Now, however, they began to back against the senate politicians or ambitious generals who promised them subsidised, or even free, corn. Violence and bloodshed became common in the decade after Catiline's defeat.

22 After the murder in 52 BCE of a politician, Clodius, who had given the urban poor free grain, mobs burned down the Senate house and killed the rich in the street. It was against this background that Julius Caesar marched his army across the Italian border and took all power into his own hands.

Italy, impoverishment of the Italian peasantry, pillaging the cities of the Roman Empire. That essentially is the base on which the Roman Empire was established.

The Roman Empire and the legacy of Spartacus

It was the basis which meant the empire could dominate the whole of the Mediterranean and Middle East area for several hundred years. Nevertheless, inbuilt into it was a contradiction. The contradiction of course was that if you fight wars to conquer more slaves, what happens when the cost of the war becomes so great, it no longer becomes worthwhile to keep the war going. In that situation, fighting war becomes a self-perpetuating thing which you can't solve. You try to solve it, and the Romans tried to solve it then by having, I hate to use the phrase about human beings, breeding slaves. That is they established slave farms. Let the slaves mate and bring up small slaves. You know, their attitude was rather like having a cattle farm. That's how their attitude was. But of course, once you do that, you have the problem. The logic of slavery in the first place was that a slave is cheap to keep because you don't have to keep the wife and the children. Once you talk in terms of the slave farm, you are talking about the cost of production of the slaves rising to the level which begins to approach the cost of production of peasants.

A central contradiction at the end of the day, the Roman Empire tried to solve it by moving over from slavery to what's called the colonate, an early form of serfdom in which the peasants were set on the land, given a bit of land and they were told they were responsible looking after the land. They had to hand half of what they produced over to the local landowners or to imperial taxation. But it didn't actually solve the problems. The secret to both the rise of the Roman Empire and the secret to the decline of the Roman Empire is built into the central feature of slavery.

You can add other features. While you have slavery, the slave has very little interest in improving the land on which he or she works. They are going to let you die in ten years time, they aren't concerned with keeping you in your old age, so why not say, just piss into the milk, don't worry about re-fertilizing the land, mistreat the animals. The whole lot. At the same time, while you had slavery, slaves were cheap. The Romans were aware of quite advanced mechanical instruments. I mean, they knew about the watermills. The watermill was established I think 100 BCE. Yet what's interesting was how sparse in reality was the use of the watermill compared with the later medieval period in Europe, which on the face of it seemed much more backward than the Roman Empire. The Romans didn't have a real interest in innovation except in the military sphere. Didn't have an interest in the Roman slaves and their in tools and therefore you have at the height of the Roman Empire, you begin to see the impoverishment of the empire. The empire can't break out.

Now the last thing, I want to return to Spartacus and to some extent to the peasant revolts, which took place under the Romans.[23] For us what's important about Spartacus is it shows that an army can fight. What I would think is also significant is that Spartacus couldn't overthrow the Roman Empire. You see, could the battle have changed history? In reality, I think, I mean I like to think that Spartacus when he was outside Rome, looked at Rome and thought, 'God what happens if I conquer Rome? How do we maintain, you know, we have the slave army. We replace the legions. We replace the Senate. How are we going to maintain this civilization which exists going? How are we going to maintain it? Can we maintain it? Well, we ourselves, we don't own any land, we're not

---

23 Look at the date – the Gracchus 130 and 120 BCE, Marius just before 100, Sulpicus in 80s, Catiline in 64, Clodius in 52. In the midst of all this, in 73 – Spartacus. But contradiction – slaves were increasingly the labour force of the empire but were not the only exploited class – peasants and urban artisans, also peoples of empire. Further, slaves were a class which had great difficulty organising itself – a 'one generation' class – people who spoke different languages – and who came from different class backgrounds – rich and poor alike enslaved after battles. It's interesting that it was a specific group of slaves, gladiators who had been trained to fight originally in armies against Rome who spearheaded the revolt.

experienced working on the land, we are military slaves. The logical way to maintain it is for us to be the owners and to enslave other people'. Continue their own mechanism [of exploitation] under another fashion. That is because Rome was built upon the basis of slavery, the logic in a certain sense, if the slave army was to be victorious it would been to continue slavery.

In a certain sense history hadn't advanced to such a point in which it's possible for an oppressed class to see overthrowing the empire and establishing itself as a new ruling class upon a higher, better form of organization of society. And therefore, the slave revolt is a heroic revolt, but at the end of the day, it couldn't come to any programme for re-organising the empire on another basis. The choice was taking Rome and becoming a new slave-owning elite, or fleeing from the Roman Empire to the peripheral areas. It was stuck at a certain point in history.[24]

That doesn't mean we shouldn't admire and enthuse about the revolt. Not just about the slave revolt, about the various peasant revolts and so on and so forth, as they show the people at the bottom always fight back. And the people they fight back against are always the same sort of people, maybe an upper class Latin accent is different to an upper class English accent, always the same sort of background, always the same sort of training. It's interesting that the British ruling class for a hundred years trained their younger members in the glories of the Roman Empire and so on and so forth. Trained them to behave as if they were Roman rulers, the same nastiness, the same cold bloodedness, the viciousness, and so on

---

[24] Finally, the central contradiction – slave production was the basis for civilisation, which could not exist without it. Choices – slave revolts in Sicily tried to set up independent slave monarchies – based on peasant production and (ex-slave ruling class). Spartacus's army faced problem – if it took Rome, how was it to stop Roman civilisation falling apart – or was it to establish new slave society with itself on top? Yet the logic of defeat of the slave revolt was eventual undermining of the Roman empire itself, once sources of new slaves dried up – an empire which could only exist through pillage and war.

and so forth.

The fightback took place. The fightback in itself couldn't change history because essentially the Roman Empire was based on slavery, because the forces of producing the livelihood of human beings was at very low level of development. The low level of development meant to have civilisation, you had to have exploitation of people on a massive scale, but the exploitation meant there wasn't any easy way which you could just overthrow that and establish a higher order of society.

People could fight back, but without at the end of the day, you know, being able to perceive any other form of organisation of society. We should learn from that because we're in a society which, you know, there's not a shortage of production, there is overproduction, massive production of wealth which people don't know what to do with under capitalism, so therefore we are in a different society, we can learn from their fightback and we can fightback with a higher aim at the end of it.

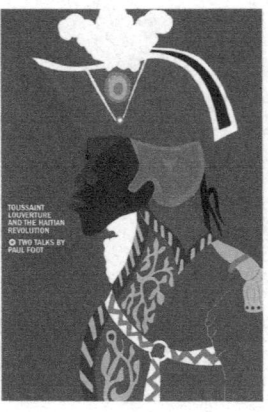

Toussaint Louverture & the Haitian Revolution

Two talks by Paul Foot

Paul Foot once declared, that the Haitian Revolution which erupted in 1791, was 'perhaps the most glorious victory of the oppressed over their oppressors in all history'. It was a world-historic event, an epic twelve year long black liberation struggle which abolished slavery for good in what was then the prized French sugar plantation colony of Saint Domingue. In 1804, the new nation of Haiti was born, the second post-colonial nation ever and the first independent black republic outside of Africa.

In two characteristically brilliant lectures, delivered in 1978 and 1991 and published here for the first time, Paul Foot made an impassioned and compelling attempt to bring home to his audience some sense of the richness of the 'hidden history' of the Haitian Revolution. Through an inspired popularisation of C.L.R. James's classic work, *The Black Jacobins*, the lectures showed the emancipation of the enslaved was fought for and won by the enslaved themselves. Yet the lectures also outline the importance of the outstanding revolutionary leadership represented by Toussaint Louverture. There are few better possible introductions to the Haitian Revolution for anti-racists and anti-imperialists today than this powerful retelling of the story of the only successful slave revolt in history.

ISBN: 9 781914 143311

a Redwords pamphlet

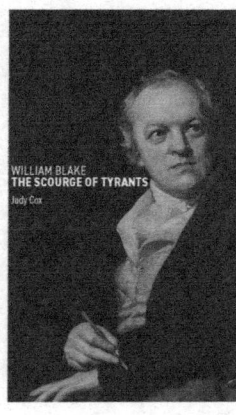

William Blake
The Scrounge of Tyrants
by Judy Cox

Revised edition

Paul Foot said this of the first edition: Judy Cox has written a wonderfully inspiring little book about Blake. She cuts away all the romantic and reactionary drivel written about him and reveals him as a prophet of liberation, political, artistic and sexual liberation. She sets him in his time as a creature of the French revolutionary fervour and expertly distinguishes him from the other great poets and writers of the enlightenment. Quite impossible to miss.

ISBN: 978 1 917020 07 7

a Redwords book

Palestinian Cultures of Resistance

by Michael Lavalette

Every great people's liberation movement also creates its distinct cultural expression – think of the black struggle in America or the Irish national struggle. Palestine is no exception and Michael Lavalette's wonderful book provides an insightful guide to Palestine's culture of resistance through the work of three of its greatest poets and its foremost visual artist. It is a pleasure and an inspiration. —**John Molyneux** (1948-2022), author of *The Dialectics of Art*).

This is the history of modern Palestine shown through the eyes of the country's poets and artists. It is a delight to read and to understand how they have been inspired by, and in turn inspired, resistance. — **Lindsey German**, Stop the War Campaign

I now live on Samos, working with and alongside refugees from across the Middle East and Asia. Together we directly witness, endure and resist the relentless cruelties and wickedness of the powerful. I have been electrified by the words and work of Kanafani, Tuqan, Darwish and al-Ali who are the focus of *Palestinian Cultures of Resistance*. They speak to the oppressed everywhere. They are inspirational, thought provoking and energising. This is the best book I have read in years. — **Chris Jones** Emeritus Prof of Social Work, Liverpool University, Refugee support worker, Samos

ISBN : 9781912926015

a Redwords book